AF497677

MEMOIR

OF

MARTHA C. THOMAS,

LATE OF

BALTIMORE,

MARYLAND.

PHILADELPHIA:

JOSEPH & WILLIAM KITE, PRINTERS.

1837.

INTRODUCTION.

THE following brief Memoir is published
in the hope that it may prove the means of
awakening, in the minds of its readers, avail-
ing desires after that blessedness, of which,
through the mercy of God in Christ Jesus,
the subject of it was happily made a parta-
ker. It adds another to the multitude of
instances already furnished, that " it is not
by works of righteousness that we have
done, but according to his mercy, he saveth
us, by the washing of regeneration and re-
newing of the Holy Ghost, which he shed
on us abundantly, through Jesus Christ, our
Saviour; that being justified by his grace,
we should be made heirs according to the
hope of eternal life."

If an amiable and lovely disposition, joined to a circumspect and innocent life, could
afford hope on a dying bed, our beloved

friend, more than most others, might have realized it. But as if to prove to all that nothing short of an interest in the crucified and risen Saviour, and that conversion of heart, through the power of the Holy Spirit, which is compared to " becoming as a little child," can stand us in stead at that trying moment, it pleased her heavenly Father to give her very humbling views of the depravity of the unregenerate heart, and of the purity and holiness necessary to be experienced before she could hope for an admittance into that celestial city, where all is light and peace, and love; and where nothing that is in the least degree defiled, can ever enter.

Great was the conflict of mind which ensued. Sensible that she was not prepared for the blessed society of saints and angels, and the spirits of the just made perfect, in the presence of God and the Lamb, the language of her agonized spirit was, " What must I do to be saved?" Seeing nothing in herself but sin and imperfection, without the ability to come out of this lost and undone condition, or even to preserve herself from still greater degrees of alienation from the perfection of the gospel, she was through mercy led to cast herself as a penitent sinner on Jesus, "the Lamb of God, who taketh away the sin of the world." Earnestly did she strive and pray to feel the pardoning efficacy of his precious blood, for past transgressions, and the renewings of his grace, that through the baptism of the Holy Ghost and fire, the power of sin might be subdued its pollution thoroughly washed away, and all things become new and all things of God.

Nor was the struggle in vain. He who gave himself for his church, and for every member of it, that he might sanctify and cleanse it with the washing of water by the word, that it should be holy and without blemish, was graciously pleased to hear and answer her prayer. That blessed Spirit of Truth, which Christ declared should not only " convince the world of sin," but " lead his disciples into all truth," and be their teacher and comforter, was pleased to work in her heart the change she longed for ; to give her a living faith, and an abiding interest in the blood of Jesus, to set her free from the law of sin and death, and translate her into the glorious liberty of the children of God.

The dawning of this new creation was a

blessed day to her soul, in which she was enabled to praise her God and Saviour, and to testify to his goodness and mercy; and though the natural diffidence of her temper, often led her to distrust her own feelings, yet as she patiently endured the turning of the Divine hand, casting herself in simple faith on the Lord's disposal, she experienced the joys of his salvation, and could triumphantly say, " death has no sting, nor will the grave have any victory."

That mercy which wrought such happy effects for her, and enabled her to meet her change in the full assurance of a glorious immortality, is freely offered for the redemption of all. " The fountain for sin and uncleanliness " is open to all mankind, and capable of making white as wool or as the snow, those whose sins may be as scarlet or the crimson dye. The compassionate Saviour is still extending his gracious invitation to " *all* that labour and are heavy laden " with the burden of sin, " Come unto me, and I will give you rest." When contemplating her own unworthiness, the greatness of the change wrought in her, and the fulness and freeness of the salvation which comes by

Christ, the Lord; the interesting subject of the following pages ardently desired that all might enjoy the blessedness of which she so richly participated might come unto Jesus, and by faith in his power, and obedience to his will, know him to become precious indeed to their souls.

May the perusal of these pages, under the blessing of the Lord, awaken to a just sense of our need of a Saviour, and lead us earnestly and devoutly to seek Him who hath declared, " Him that cometh unto me, I will in no wise cast out."

MEMOIR

OF

MARTHA C. THOMAS.

MARTHA C. THOMAS was born 5th Month, 13th, 1805. Her parents, James and Martha Carey, of Baltimore, were members of the Society of Friends. She was early remarkable for a quietness of manner, and steadiness of deportment, much beyond her years. She also evinced an unusual timidity and diffidence, which continued with her through life. About the age of twelve years, she was sent to a boarding school in Montgomery County, Maryland. She felt the separation from her family acutely, suffering so

much from depression of spirits, that there is
no doubt it exercised a very unfavorable influence on many of the subsequent years of
her life.

Finding that she did not become recon-
ciled to absence from home, her parents
sent for her before the expiration of a year,
and her education was finished under their
roof.

It is not intended to follow her through
the days of her youth. To speak of the
character of her mind, and of her deportment, more nearly comports with the design
of this notice. Endued with an acuteness of
sensibility which amounted almost to a morbid
affection, joined to a distrust of self, and a disposition to look upon the dark side of the pic-
ture, she was sometimes reduced to a state
of despondency, amounting to little less than
melancholy. Generous and disinterested in
her disposition, she preferred the gratifica-
tion of others to her own; and such were
the integrity and decision of her character,
adorned by unobtrusive modesty and sweet-
ness of manner, that she was rarely led by
persuasion or example to swerve from the
path of strict propriety, into which she had

been introduced by a very careful and pious mother.

Before she was twenty years of age, her affectionate heart was deeply tried by the dangerous illness of her father, to whom she was tenderly attached. Feeling that his loss would almost destroy her earthly comforts, she watched over him with the most anxious and assiduous care. His life was at that time spared, but similar attacks of violent disease to which he was afterwards liable, kept her tremblingly alive to the precarious tenure of his existence, and contributed to cloud her spirits.

In 1830, after an acquaintance of several years, she was married to Dr. Richard H. Thomas, of Baltimore. Amid the cares of a family, and the new train of affections thus called into action, she soon lost much of the gloom that had clouded the morning of her life. She remained under her father's roof, and had an opportunity of continuing those filial duties to her beloved parents, which had long been her pleasure, while at the same time she fulfilled the obligations of a tender wife, and of a devoted mother.

In 1832, when cholera made its appearance in Baltimore, she was in the country with her sick infant. She insisted upon returning to town and remaining with her husband, choosing rather to encounter the risk of taking the disease, than to be absent from him when she thought he was in danger.

Continuing in the faithful discharge of her various duties, encouraging her husband in the responsibilities of an arduous profession, and cheering the declining years of her parents, she was as happy as virtue, love, kind friends, and prosperity could make her. But it was not the design of her Maker that she should rest in these things for happiness.

We have said that her duties as a daughter, wife, and mother, were carefully performed. She was also kind to her domestics, easy of access to her friends and to the poor; regularly attended religious meetings, read her bible, and enjoyed the company of the serious. Dignity and propriety marked her actions; she was amiable and benevolent,—in the eyes of the world she was good. But He who has declared " there is none good," no, not one, and that " except a man be born again, he cannot see the kingdom of God," saw fit to awaken her to a sense of her undone condition, without him, and to show her that a life even of great comparative innocence and circumspection, is not a safe ground on which to trust our hopes of heaven, without an interest in the blood of Jesus, and that change of heart which is produced by the cleansing and sanctifying baptism of the Holy Spirit.

From an early period of life, she had been favored with seasons of precious visitation, in which her heart was tendered by the love of God, and desires raised after holiness and heaven. But, as she expressed with sorrow to the writer of these lines, she too easily permitted the engagements of the moment, or the anticipation of the future, to divert her attention from these religious impressions, deferring the entire surrender of her heart until a more convenient season, though with a full resolution that at some time she would make a decided stand. Delay produced irresolution, and thus years passed on without her salvation being any nearer than when she first believed herself called. While speaking of these affecting recollections, during her last illness, she lamented over the procrastination and indifference which so much abounded, observing that if people could but see things while in health, as they did when laid on the bed of death, they would dread to delay a moment.

How long the disposition to put off the work of salvation might have prevailed with her, if health had continued, we know not, but the Lord, who in kindness had marked her for his own, gently laid upon her the hand of disease.

In the merciful dispensations of an all-wise Providence, He is often pleased to make use of sickness as a means of promoting spiritual health, and to teach the invalid and her friends lessons of instruction, which, in the buoyancy of health and prosperity, pass unheeded, or make but transient impressions on the mind. These seasons of pain and languor, in which the mind is withdrawn from the busy pursuits or pleasures of life, and an eternal world, with all its solemn realities, brought nearer to our view, are among our choicest blessings, though in disguise.

The sympathies excited for the sufferer; the increased affection which is the usual consequence of the attentions t ey require; the absence of every inducement to deceive, and the consciousness that we must ere long, part with the beloved object of our solicitude and care, are all calculated to seal with a deep and lasting impress those admonitions which fall from the dying lips of a friend.

The instance before us is one of affecting interest—the Lord grant that, as he has been pleased mercifully to redeem our departed friend, and to take her to himself as with a song of praise and triumph, his gracious purposes toward her surviving friends may also be fulfilled; and her early and lamented removal from a circle where she was eminently beloved, be blessed as a means of inciting others to press after that living, sanctifying faith, in a crucified Redeemer, which was her victory over the world, death, and the grave.

In the summer of 1834, she was attacked with a cough, which, though not alarming in its character, resisted the ordinary remedies. It was much increased by exposure in the 10th month, and the death of her father, after an illness of several weeks, with the fatigue and anxiety attendant upon nursing

him, contributed to fix a disease already
threatening. This bereavement was a heavy
blow, which she ceased not to feel. She
passed a long and severe winter in her chamber, enduring much from disease and from
painful remedies. In the spring of 1835, as
her cough still continued, she was strongly ad-
vised by her physicians to try the effects of
a sea voyage. She had a great dread of the
ocean, and felt very reluctant to leave her
two little boys and her aged mother, whose
health was very infirm. She yielded however
to the solicitations of her friends, under the impression that it was her duty; though at the
same time she believed it would be unavailing.

On the 8th of 5th month, 1835, she embark-
ed with her husband on board the ship Roscoe,
at New York, for Liverpool. The meek re-
signation and composure of her mind, in
entering on this engagement, were instructive.
In conversation with a friend, she mentioned
in affecting terms, the trial she had passed
through, in parting from her family, and the
consciousness that her disease was beyond
the reach of remedial means—yet that she
thought it right to yield for the sake of her
beloved connexions. In allusion to her dread

of the sea, she said she scarcely dared to
think of it, but was striving to cast herself
on the Lord for support and protection. This
she was favoured to do in the simplicity of
a child, and He sustained her. Her fear of
the sea was removed, and from that time
she was preserved in tranquillity and comfort
even under circumstances most likely to
alarm. The voyage to England, though it
occupied but seventeen days, was beneficial
to her, and she was able on landing to attend
Friends' meeting for worship, at Liverpool.
Several months were spent in travelling lei-
surely through England, France and Ireland,
during which she was never once tempted
to visit any place of public amusement, however attractive, on any pretext of its being innocent and allowable in travellers.
From the period when her cough became serious, her conscientiousness, which had always
been great, increased ; and as her hold upon
this life loosened, her thoughts seemed to
dwell much upon that which is to come,
and she began earnestly to seek the kingdom
of Heaven. While in Europe, she saw
many palaces, castles, and princely domains
of noblemen and kings. Though their splen-

dour and magnificence struck her with
surprise, the prevailing sentiment of her
mind was " all is vanity;" feeling how utterly
impotent are all such things to procure for.
man true happiness. The mildness and dignity of her manner, joined to her obviously
delicate health, gained her many friends
abroad, for whose kindness she always continued to feel grateful.

The voyage home was a long one, and
attended with severe storms, in one of which
the ship was struck by a squall, and two
large spars were carried away by the vio-
lence of the gale. In the confusion and
uproar of the moment, she was calm and
self-possessed, and contributed much by her
manner to allay the alarm of her fellow
passengers. Her own words will best ex-
plain her conduct on this occasion. In
answer to an inquiry if she had felt afraid
of the sea ; she observed, " Dreadfully so ; I
felt almost as if I had rather die than go to sea.
But when I went on ship board, I endeavored
to cast myself entirely upon the protection of
the Lord ; and all fear was taken away
from me, even during the most violent storm.
I felt awful it is true, but my mind was stay-

ed; and I recur with pleasure to the sweet assurance of his superintending providence, with which I was frequently favored, while at sea."

On her arrival in New York, in the 9th month, she was met by the afflicting intelligence of the death of her youngest son. The blow was as severe as it was sudden and unexpected, but she sustained it with much fortitude, resigning all her fondly cherished anticipations of beholding him improved in intelligence and beauty, if not without a struggle, at least without a murmur. Her health seemed much benefitted by the voyage and travel, and she cherished the hope that she might now be permitted to remain at that beloved home which she had before so reluctantly left. But here again she was disappointed. As the winter approached, she began to decline, and her physicians pronounced a southern climate to be indispensable. To this advice she decidedly objected. Unwilling as she was to leave home, she at the same time expressed a conviction that it would not restore her health; that it would subject her husband and herself to great sacrifices, and after all,

end in disappointment. She begged to be
allowed to die at home. She, however,
again yielded to the earnest solicitations of
her anxious friends, and consented to the
voyage, in the belief that it might be her
duty. With a heavy heart and sad forebo-
dings, she left home once more, on the 3d of
the 11th month, in company with her husband, child, and sister-in-law. Soon after
reaching St. Augustine in Florida, they dis-
covered that the climate did not answer the
flattering account they had received of it.
So far from being uniformly mild and plea-
sant, it was very changeable and not unfre-
quently raw and damp. A violent cold,
which was contracted here, reduced her
very low; at the same time the town was
threatened with an attack by the Indians,
who approached within a few miles, burning
the houses, and killing the inhabitants. Under
these very trying circumstances she remained several weeks, her disorder daily becoming worse, with no way of escape from the
place, except by returning northward, at
the imminent risk of aggravating all her
symptoms. Providentially she was enabled
o leave St. Augustine early in the 1st month,

1836, in a steam-boat which touched there for wood, on her way to Mobile. She suffered much from high fever and exhaustion, during a voyage of six days to Key West; having narrowly escaped destruction by a fire which occurred at night, while the boat was at anchor and all hands asleep. At Key West she grew worse, the hectic fever being violent, and her prostration extreme. The weather was unusually cold; the house had no fire-place or chimney in it; and she could with difficulty be kept at all comfortable. The accommodations, though the best in the place, were very poor; and diet suitable for an invalid, was hardly to be procured. All these deprivations she endured with patience and submission. As her health continued to decline, she was led to take a nearer view of death than she had yet done, and to examine the ground upon which her hopes of acceptance rested.

It had been more than a year since she had been earnestly engaged to seek the kingdom of heaven; her walk had been scrupulously correct, and in the eyes of her friends, she had become a changed and pious woman. But her own opinion of her

spiritual condition was very different. She
felt herself to be a sinner, the subject of
condemnation and of wrath, but for the inter-
position of a Saviour. She ardently desired
to realize an interest in him, as her Redeemer—to know her sins forgiven, and experience that " acceptance in the beloved " without which she felt that she must be miserable. The want of these blessings occasioned
her to mourn as one who will not be com-
forted. Deep and distressing were her conflicts. She bewailed herself as a reprobate,
and was reduced almost to despondency.
Earnestly as she sought the blessing, it nevertheless pleased the Father of mercies to
withhold from her, for a season, the conso-
lations of his Gospel. Let not any who
may be introduced into the like conflicts, be
discouraged by this account, for as they are
faithful and patiently wait the Lord's time, they
will at length come to experience, as she did,
that " the deeper sinners mourn for their Saviour, the deeper he makes them drink of the
cup of salvation at his appearing." Blessed
are they who greatly hunger and thirst after
righteousness, for they shall certainly be fill-

ed, according to the degree of their emptiness, in the Lord's own time.

. After very severe suffering from the disease, by which she was brought to the brink of the grave, she was able, in the 2d month, to get across to Cuba. The congenial temperature and balmy atmosphere of this Island contributed much to recruit her health; and she was favoured to pass two months in comparative comfort and much quiet, in a private house in the suburbs of Havanna. Most of her time was spent in reading the bible, and a few religious books, and in striving for the blessing she so earnestly desired.

On the first of the 5th month, she was permitted to return to that beloved home which at one period she hardly dared to hope she should again see. Though her life was now evidently drawing to its close, she thanked God and took courage, resolving, with divine assistance, to centre all her hopes in eternity, and to strive without ceasing for that blessed assurance which she believed to be the privilege of every christian. As the summer advanced, it was evident to her religious friends that the good seed which had been sown in her heart by the great Husbandman, had taken root, was growing apace, and promised to become a flourishing tree, notwithstanding the obstructions which the doubts and fears of her timid disposition, threw in its way. Her state of mind, about this time, was a very interesting one. Earnestly engaged in seeking that pearl which she prized above all price, at times she believed herself almost in possesion of it; then the sense of her own unworthiness would press heavily upon her spirits, and lead her to doubt whether it could be so. Thus she seemed like one who having just escaped from bondage, can scarcely believe that he is free.

About the last of the 8th month, as her husband entered the room where she sat reading the bible, she said, "Doctor, I have been looking for something I had no right to expect; some supernatural intimation of my acceptance, a light from heaven as in the case of the Apostle Paul, or something like it. I find now that I have only to believe, and leave the rest to my Saviour, and He will, in his own time, grant me the assurance of acceptance and pardon, which I have so long sought in vain, because

I looked for it in my own time and way."
Her path was now comparatively plain
and her progress in best things proportion-
ally great. She was enabled to cast her
care upon Him who cared for her, without,
in the meantime, relaxing her exertions to
serve and love him.

The autumn was unusually cold, and in the
9th month she was mostly confined to her
chamber. Although her health continued
about the same as it had been for some time
previous, she spoke and acted as if she believed her departure to be at hand. After
making such arrangements for the care of
her little boy as she approved, she appeared
to give him entirely up—spake much of
her approaching departure, and expressed a
lively hope that she should be enabled,
through mercy, to give in her account with
joy and not with sorrow. She was favored
at seasons through this month to experience
sweet peace and comfort in the Holy Ghost,
while at others " the enemy seemed to come
in like a flood, to use her own expression,
and swallow up all her comforts." But blessed be Emanuel's name, " she was brought
low and he helped her." The burden of her

exercise and the blessing she most craved was, that she might be permitted to sit with acceptance at the feet of Jesus, and hear the gracious words which proceed out of his mouth. " Lord, said she, I desire to lay very low at thy feet. Oh, admit me into thy kingdom, if it be to take the very lowest place."

Such was the state of her mind at the approach of yearly meeting which commenced the last of the 10th month. Several of the valued friends who attended it, visited her sick room. The comfort and encouragement which they were enabled to impart to her exercised spirit, cheered and strengthened her. The love and christian fellowship which united her to them, she frequently mentioned with a grateful heart. The animating thought seemed often to refresh her spirit, that if the love and fellowship of the saints be so sweet on earth, it must be much more so in heaven. The company and religious communications of these dear friends appeared to have a sustaining influence and contributed, under the divine blessing, to assure her of that change of heart and spiritual advancement which her natural diffidence and self-distrust often caused her

to fear she had not fully witnessed.   In a
conversation with one of them she expressed
her abiding sense of her own unworthiness,
and of the mercy of God in Christ Jesus,
her Saviour, saying, " my only hope and
trust is in him, and in his precious blood.
He died for sinners.   He is indeed precious
to me, yet I feel myself so poor and unworthy that I am sometimes tempted to fear
he will not receive me at last."   Her friend
cited to her the many precious promises
made in Holy Scripture to such as were
earnestly seeking the Lord, and endeavored
to encourage her to look in faith to Him
who is the refuge of the poor, and the un-
failing helper of those who have no might of
their own.   Several of those passages appeared to afford her consolation, and she
expressed the humble hope that she should
be supported in the last hour of conflict, of
which she had naturally a great dread.
The power of the Holy Spirit to enable us
to triumph over the infirmities of nature, and
the blessed presence of the Captain of Salvation, with his faithful followers, in that trying season, being adverted to, she seemed
animated with the prospect, and her faith re-

newed, in the belief that he would be graciously near to sustain her departing spirit.

Before parting, she observed, " I am dead to the world now, as it is to me. I never took as much delight in dress as some, though I paid too much attention to it. To me it is now all vanity; but there is one thing I should like to do, if I am able. I would wish to put on a plain dress, and be carried to meeting, and sit there as long as I could, as a testimony in favor of plainness. It can make no difference as to my poor self, but perhaps it might be an encouragement to some others to dress more consistently." She was told the enfeebled state of her body would render this exertion impracticable, and that where the will was surrendered to the Lord's disposal, it was often accepted instead of the deed. She replied that she was entirely given up to go, and much desired it; but if her friends thought her unable, she was disposed to yield to their judgment, though she wished all to know her sentiments on the subject of dress.

She remarked that she had been tenderly visited by the Holy Spirit from an early period of her childhood, and could look back to many precious seasons which she had enjoyed, but had to lament her frequent feeling of indifference to religious things, occasioned by not duly regarding those visitations of Divine love, and suffering her mind to be too much taken up with other things. Though she had had some heavenly meetings, in which she enjoyed the presence of her Saviour, yet by indulging her thoughts in wandering, she had often found it hard work to come to that state of quiet settlement and waiting, in which true worship was performed; adding, " Ah, how very differently do these things appear at such a time as this—when in health we are too thoughtless and negligent of them; but when sickness and death are near, we see them to be of infinite moment. I wish it were in my power to warn all my young friends to prize their time while in health, and seriously ponder these things."

On the evening of the second of eleventh month, she was seized with nervous twitchings and such a sense of sinking, as induced her to believe she was dying. With great composure she desired her husband, who was at the time engaged with a com-

mittee of the yearly meeting, might not be
sent for, saying " I have given him up to the
service of the Lord. You know he that
loveth husband or wife more than me, is not
worthy of me." To the question how she felt,
she replied, " I feel very peaceful. My work
is done. There is nothing for me to do. It
is time for me to go. My hopes are based
upon that rock which cannot be moved."
She expressed great affection for her family
and friends; indeed her heart seemed to
overflow with love. To a dear relative she
said, " Oh, my dear, I beseech thee, turn thy
attention to serious things. Thou art now
very much taken up with the world; I trust it
will not always be so. You must all come
to this." "If this be death, I feel very
peaceful—all is sweet peace." Her husband
coming in and expressing his belief that
she would soon be better, she received the
information with the same calmness she had
manifested throughout. After laying down,
she was earnestly engaged in supplication
for him and their son, commending them
into the Lord's hand. She continued the
next day very peaceful, having been favored
as she believed to cast all her burden

upon the Lord, and having arranged all her worldly concerns, she apparently dismissed them from her mind.

From this period she lived but a day at a time, regarding each one as the last, and waiting the Lord's time, in humble and child-like reliance that it would be the best. Meanwhile she was not idle, but leaving the things which were behind, she "pressed forward towards the mark for the prize of the high calling of God, in Christ Jesus." With all the peace and comfort she enjoyed through faith in her Saviour, her humility and self-abasement were great. To a friend who said to her, "If thou hast any advice to give, I shall be glad to receive it;" she answered, "I am too poor a creature to give any one advice, I can only direct thee to the same Fountain, it is equally open to all."

It would be impossible to convey in words an adequate idea of the holy tranquillity which prevailed in her apartment. Death so completely robbed of its terrors, through the power of a crucified Redeemer, frequently formed the subject of conversation, in which she joined with composure and interest. She had learned to contemplate it as a change rather to be desired than feared. Let none suppose that this state of mind was brought about by bodily suffering or weariness of life. Far from it. The former she had been mercifully spared, and the latter she never experienced. On the contrary, she said to a friend, "I have every thing to live for;" and to her husband, "I often think how much happier we should now be, if my life was continued, than we have ever been before;" alluding to her change of heart and evidence of acceptance. On the 8th of the 11th month she rode out for the last time. Being alone with her in the carriage, her husband inquired, "If the choice were allowed thee to be restored to health or to depart, what would be thy decision?" "I would not hesitate, said she, I would rather depart. My peace is now made, and I don't know that it would ever be the case again."

On the morning of the 10th, after a time of great oppression, in which those about her thought she was dying, her desire for the spiritual welfare of one who had come from a distance to see her, seemed to triumph over the weakness of her frame; her other attendants having withdrawn from the bed, she addressed her friend who leaned over her. She could not raise her voice above a whisper, but her manner was so impressive, that her words seemed to have a sensible power —they were more than felt, it was as if they could be touched and handled. She said, " I am very glad thou came—I was afraid I should never see thee again in this world." Then closing her eyes as if communing with the Holy Spirit, she continued,* " I wish to press upon thee, the importance of religion. I feel great concern for thee. I want to entreat thee to seek an interest in thy Saviour,—come to him in humility and faith, determined to know nothing but Jesus Christ and him crucified. I have been afraid, [this she said with great tenderness,] that thy trials, instead of making thee humble, have raised a rebellious spirit. This is wrong, oh, very wrong. Thou canst never know true happiness until thou givest up to the influence of the Holy Spirit. Come to the foot of the cross. I was long trying in my own strength, but it would not do. I had to

* This is all given in the words of the friend to whom it was addressed.

throw myself at the foot of the cross. If thou couldst only once experience the peace which the assurance of acceptance gives, thou wouldst find it greater happiness than all the riches and pleasures of this world can bestow. Only come to the foot of the cross. I feel great concern on thy account. I fear thou art so much taken up with this world, that thou doest not think as much of best things as thou oughtest. I want thee to turn thy whole mind, soul, and spirit to the great work, it is of more importance than any worldly concern. I hope we shall meet in Heaven, all join our dear father there, and be a family of love in Heaven." Her friend said, "pray for me, that it may be so." She replied, "I have many times been deeply exercised, both on thy account and that of dear J——s. I do desire it for you more than any earthly good—far more, for what is every thing else in comparison; it is dust in the balance."

Her exercise of mind, on account of several others of her friends, was equally great, —she was enabled to plead with them in love, and experienced that peace which always follows the performance of religious duty. Every day seemed to add to her growth in grace, and in the knowledge of Christ. Many remarks indicative of her entire reliance upon her Saviour, were omitted to be recorded. Indeed it was not until a few days before her decease that memorandums were regularly made. Most of the following are nearly in her own words. Much that was said to others has been lost, but it is believed that enough has been preserved to evidence the ground of her hopes and their power to sustain a mind naturally timid, desponding and full of self-distrust.

2nd day, 14th of 11th month: She said, "Satan has buffetted me to-day very sorely. Thou hast no idea, how hard I have had to hold on: Sometimes he seems almost ready to snatch me away, but my Saviour-holds me."

3rd day, 15th. At an early hour her husband was awakened by her voice. She was repeating some portions of Scripture. "Oh death where is thy sting! oh grave where is thy victory? The sting of death is sin, but thanks be to God who giveth us the victory through our Lord Jesus Christ." "Lord now lettest thou thy servant depart in peace, for mine eyes have seen thy salvation." Finding her husband awake, she said: "Oh husband I have had such a peaceful, happy night by myself: I have wished I had a christian friend by me that I might talk of heaven. How wonderful to think that so poor, unworthy and miserable a creature as I am, should go to heaven, to be so happy." Being reminded of the change which had been wrought in her by the power of Divine Grace, she added, "Oh yes! washed and made white in the blood of the Lamb, his precious blood. I want all my friends to go to heaven.

> " You need not one be left behind,
> For Christ hath died for all mankind."

She then repeated the following hymn:

> Come, thou fount of every blessing,
>   Tune my heart to sing thy grace,
> Streams of mercy never ceasing
>   Call for songs of loudest praise:
> Teach me some melodious sonnet,
>   Sung by flaming tongues above:
> Praise the mount—O fix me on it,
>   Mount of God's unchanging love.

Here I raise my Ebenezer,
  Hither by thy help I'm come;
And I hope by thy good pleasure,
  Safely to arrive at home:
Jesus sought me when a stranger,
  Wandering from the fold of God;
He, to save my soul from danger,
  ·Interpos'd his precious blood.

O! to grace how great a debtor
  Daily I'm constrained to be!
Let that grace, Lord, like a fetter,
  Bind my wandering heart to thee!
Prone to wander, Lord, I feel it;
  Prone to leave the God I love—
Here's my heart, Lord, take and seal it,
  Seal it from thy courts above.

Being asked if she felt happy, she replied,
"yes I feel happy—I feel blissful. I believe if
it were my Saviour's will to take me now, I
should go to glory. I have had these happy
frames for a day at a time; and then again it
is as much as I can do to hold on, and I have
feared I should be lost at last. I desire to
have my lamp full of oil and trimmed, my
lamp burning, ready to enter in with the
bridegroom when he cometh, and to have
the door barred after me." Though very
feeble in body, her mind continued peaceful
and calm through the day. Her impression

on getting into bed at night was that she should not rise out of it again. Being asked how she felt, she replied, " Tranquil." " I commend thee," said her friend, " to him who is able to keep thee," she added, " body, soul and spirit."

4th day. To her little boy she said; " Mother has not had so comfortable · a night. She fears she was impatient." When told it had not been observed, she replied, " I fear that I have felt impatient; but I pray that I may be forgiven and that my patience may hold out."

This afternoon she had an alarming paroxysm of oppression which she bore with great patience. She believed herself to be dying. Being asked if she felt her mind stayed? she answered, " As much so I believe as my trying circumstances will permit." Desiring to be very still, she sat in silence for some time. " Oh, she began, what an unspeakable blessing to have kind friends to stick by one to the last, and then to be permitted to fall asleep in Christ, and wake with him in Heaven, and sing hallelujah, to his blessed name." A little afterward, to her husband who was sitting alone by her side, " My dear, it is an awful thing to die. The sting of death is sin.

Oh what a blessed thing to be upon the right foundation—Jesus Christ, the only foundation. What would be my condition now but for this hope. It is an awful thing to die; my natural fear of death is very great." A hope was expressed that that fear had been taken away; she said, " my Saviour has promised to be with me through the dark valley of the shadow of death; and he will be with me, I know he will be with me; I feel the ever-lasting arms to be underneath." After a few moments she proceeded; " Mercy! what a sweet word: it is so great a mercy to think I shall be saved, that I am tempted sometimes to think it impossible; Satan tried hard to-day to persuade me it was impossible I should be saved." " Tell him" said her friend, " Jesus Christ came not to call the righteous, but sinners to repentance"—and again " Christ died to save sinners of whom I am chief." " He knows that, said she, as well as I do; but I told him I would hold on—dear B—— told me to hold fast, and I will hold on; pray that I may hold on; Satan has tempted me very much these three days." A little afterwards, " I love my dear friends very much, but I want words to express how supremely I love my Saviour. Oh that they may have his support in the trying hour.   What is that sweet hymn about trials:

> ' Trials make the promise sweet,
>   Trials add new life to prayer;
> Trials bring me to his feet,
>   Lay me low and keep me there.' "

After she laid down at night she was asked if she thought she could get some sleep : " I shall sleep in glory ; said she, I have given up every thing into his blessed hands :"— " Who is able to keep that thou hast committed unto him against that day," was added.   " Yes !" said she.

5th day, 17th.   She passed a trying night, the difficulty of breathing being at times very distressing.   She repeatedly prayed that her patience might hold out. " Lord let me depart in peace, if it be thy blessed will; nevertheless not my will but thine be done." She expressed a fear, no doubt excited by the paroxysms of great oppression, that her final struggle would be agonizing ; but added, " be with me, Lord, I pray thee ; thou art strength in great weakness, and a present helper in every needful time."

This morning during one of these spells,

her sister inquired if her mind was stayed? she replied, " Oh yes," and hearing her little boy's voice; asked to see him, saying " I have given him up; it was a hard struggle, but I have given him up entirely." " An evidence, said her sister, of the powerful effects of grace on the heart." " Yes, said she, I hardly thought it possible at one time." In the afternoon she observed, " I fear I shall feel too anxious to depart. Lord keep me in perfect patience and perfect submission. I desire to say not my will but thine be done. ' Lord God Almighty, just and true are all thy ways, thou king of saints.' " She requested her friends to remain with her to the last, adding, " I know that my Redeemer will". About nine P. M. appearing to sink very fast, she desired great quiet might be preserved in the room and no agitation given way to. " It will increase my sufferings to witness the agitation of my friends; not even my dear husband must give way to any."

After remaining very tranquil for a little while, she looked up and said with a smile, " Oh what a blessing if the Lord would only keep me in this sweet quiet." Some of the family rising to leave the room, she inquired why they left her. "I thought you told me I was dying : I thought I was going to glory and I hoped the conflict would soon be over."

6th day, 16th. Contrary to our expectation, she not only survived the night, but was favored to pass it pretty comfortably, having slept at intervals in the chair. After one of the turns of oppression she said, "He hides a shining face, behind a frowning providence —he hides a shining face." "I hoped before this have waked in glory."

In the morning she remarked to her husband, "My dear, I desire to deepen every day: not to slacken in my efforts after greater faith and greater patience, because there may seem to be some improvement in my symptoms." After some ejaculatory petitions, "I am almost afraid, lest I may some times take my Maker's name in vain. But my heart is so filled with love to him, that his name is continually in my thoughts and on my tongue." To a friend who, in allusion to a preparation for death, remarked in her hearing that some persons seemed to have very little to do; she shook her head and said, "That has not been my case—no one can tell the deep baptisms, conflicts and temptations, I have had to pass through."

She was much engaged in supplication during the day, and on several occasions was remarkably drawn out in vocal prayer to her own comfort and that of her friends; one of her sisters preserved the following. "Oh Lord thou hast been pleased to spare me another day of probation. Continue I beseech thee, to sustain me by thy Divine presence, to resist the enemy of my soul's salvation, who still endeavors to deprive me of my hold on thee, my Saviour; making use of every opportunity to afflict my poor soul, to weaken my faith in thee and in thy precious promises. Oh Lord, I pray thee, be near me, as thou hast promised. Feeling myself to be a poor worm of the dust, with no might or power of my own, I humbly beseech thee to increase my faith—yes, dear Lord, increase my faith. My Saviour, who hast died for me and shed thy precious blood to redeem me—Oh, precious Jesus, enable me to cling to thy cross as a blessed refuge in this hour of trial: remove from me the fear of death if it be thy will. We acknowledge, in thy dispensations,

thy wonderful mercy to us as a family:
unite us I pray thee in serving thee with
willing minds, and finally bring us to meet
again, a family in heaven, eternally to praise
thee.   Bless all the human family, merciful
Lord, by bringing them to thee, and enable
thy poor unworthy servant to hold out to the
end, for Christ's sake—Amen."

Her aged mother, who was soon afterward
supported into the room, asking if she felt
peaceful? she answered, "I have seasons of
great peace, and assurance, if I can only
hold out to the end." Her mother replied "I
believe thou wilt."   "Dear mother, said she,
in a low whisper, she is ripe for the garner;"
and to a friend near her, "Jesus can make a
dying bed feel soft as downy pillows are."

After an alarming paroxysm she said to
her husband, "I am endeavoring to keep my
mind stayed." "There is but one thing needful," he continued, "And *Martha* has chosen
that good part which shall not be taken away
from her." "Oh," said she; "Poor Martha
was careful and troubled about many things;
but she was accepted at last; Jesus loved
Martha." "And so wilt thou be accepted I
trust," said her husband. "I hope so," she
added, "and a sweet hope it is."

7th day, 19th. She had a very distressing
night, with almost continual oppression,
but not a murmur escaped her. She requested some of the Psalms to be read,
which she much enjoyed; and it may here
be remarked, that her delight in reading
the sacred volume sensibly increased as she
was enabled to apply the blessed promises to
herself and her condition. To her husband she
said, " Pray for me that I may be favored to
depart in great peace, so that to my latest hour
I may be able to testify to the world what the
Lord has done for my poor soul. I say but
little, but I am hourly engaged in supplication, that my faith may hold out to the end,
and that the everlasting arms may be underneath." This day had been a very distressing one to her, though her mind had continued sweetly stayed.

1st day, 20th. The last night was the most
trying one she has passed, and her sufferings
were borne with lamb-like patience.

About 12 o'clock she said " Dear Saviour
had I not committed body, soul and spirit
into thy hands, what would become of me on
such a night as this. Lord if it be thy will
let me now depart in great peace: I ask in

submission." In the morning she said to a friend, "I have had a most trying night—I cannot describe the agony I suffered in one of the spells. Pray for me that I may be spared such another." To her husband, "Oh my dear, my faith almost failed me last night; pray for me that my faith may hold out to the end."

A little afterward she herself prayed fervently as follows: "Oh Lord be with me, I beseech thee, in this trying hour—suffer not my faith to fail—be thou my strength in great weakness; I have no strength or might of my own: and Oh Lord, if it be thy will let me depart I pray thee in great peace. Thou hast promised to be with me through the valley of the shadow of death, and I know thou wilt be with me. Oh sustain me by thy power, and finally receive me into thy kingdom."

Shortly afterwards she remarked, " my mind would be very comfortable, but for my bodily distress." One of her friends having said in her hearing, " Martha's faith almost failed her last night;" she rejoined, " not my faith but my heart and my flesh." As the day advanced she grew weaker, and it was evident to herself and to all, that her hour was come. About four o'clock she sent for her little son, asked to kiss him, saying "farewell! dear boy, may the Lord bless and preserve thee." She conversed with composure, with such of her friends as came in, inquiring after their families, but desired to be excused from talking much, on account of great weakness. A little before 5 o'clock she said, "I am dying, but I know you all very well." Throughout the solemn and affecting scene which preceded her peaceful close, her calmness and self-possession were strikingly evidenced by the general tenor of her remarks as well as by several occurrences. Turning to her husband, she said, "Doctor I am dying; am I not?" he replied, "My dear, I believe thou art." She added, "Pray for me—Lord Jesus be with me ; let thy poor servant now depart in great peace." She again requested that we should continue in supplication for her, on which a dear friend who sat by, remarked, "it is our duty always to pray and not to faint."— "Oh !" replied·she, with a sweet smile, "but I am always fainting." "Yes," returned her friend, "but you do not let go your confidence." "No! she continued, I cannot let go that." After a short silence she exclaimed with great solemnity, "Praise the Lord. Oh I am happy now—glory—glory —glory—precious Jesus—blessed be the Lord God—hallelujah—hallelujah—hallelujah!—pray! pray to Jesus; I feel his preence in this very room—Lord Jesus be with me." Thus she continued calling on her Saviour whom she declared to be very precious to her; and again broke forth with the language, "Now is the time, pray that I may go now. Come, blessed Jesus, come quickly! Oh, come now, blessed Lord." Supplicating still more earnestly to be released, her husband told her she must wait the Lord's own time, which would not be long. "Oh yes," she said, "Thy will, Oh Lord, be done."— Again: "Lord Jesus receive my spirit;" and presently after, "Come Lord Jesus." These were her last words. In a few minutes more she had ceased to breathe, without a groan or a struggle, resigning her spirit into the hands of that Saviour who had redeemed it by his blood and prepared it to join in the song of the Church triumphant; "Blessing and honor, and glory and power, be unto Him that sitteth upon the throne, and unto the Lamb for ever and ever."

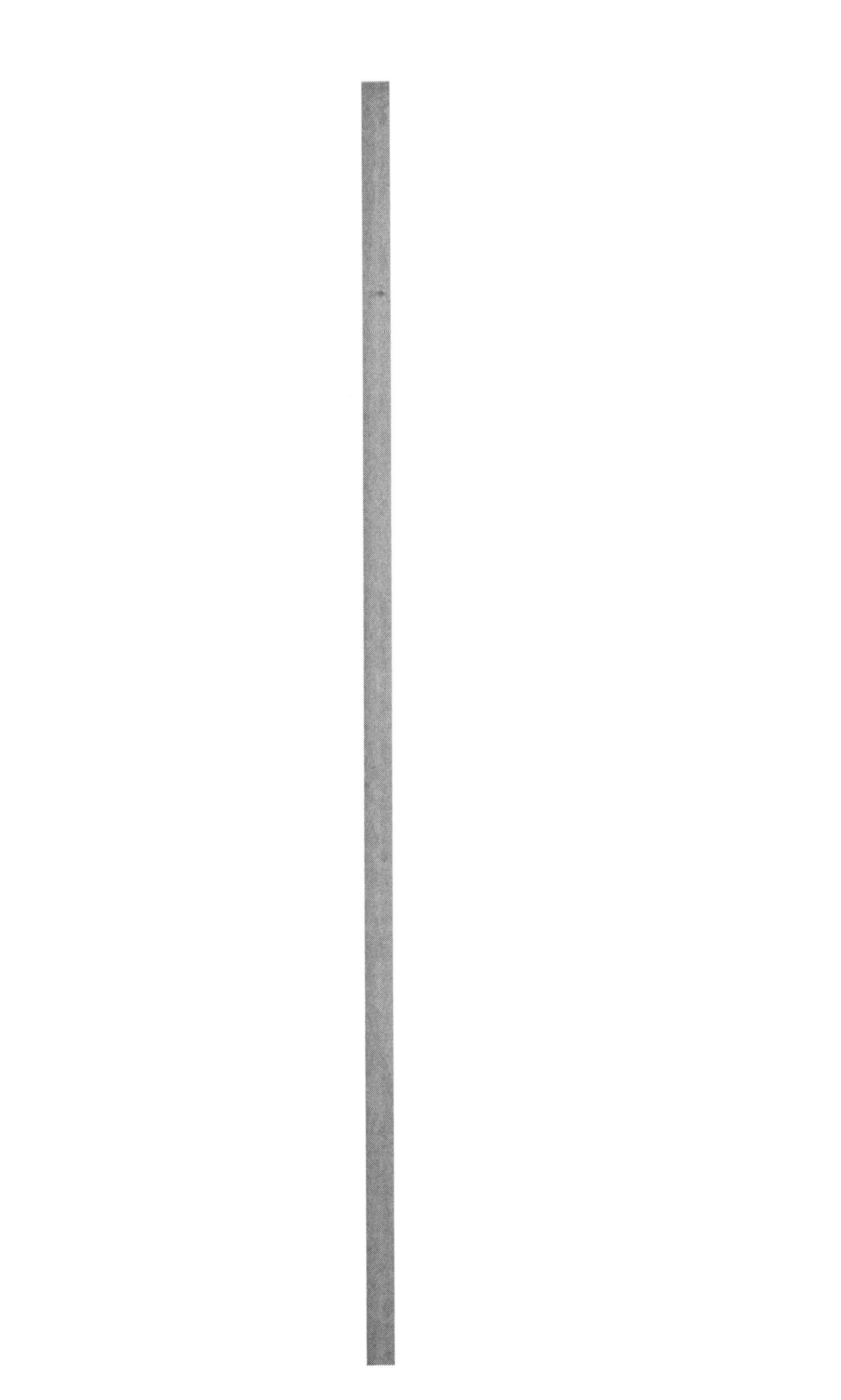

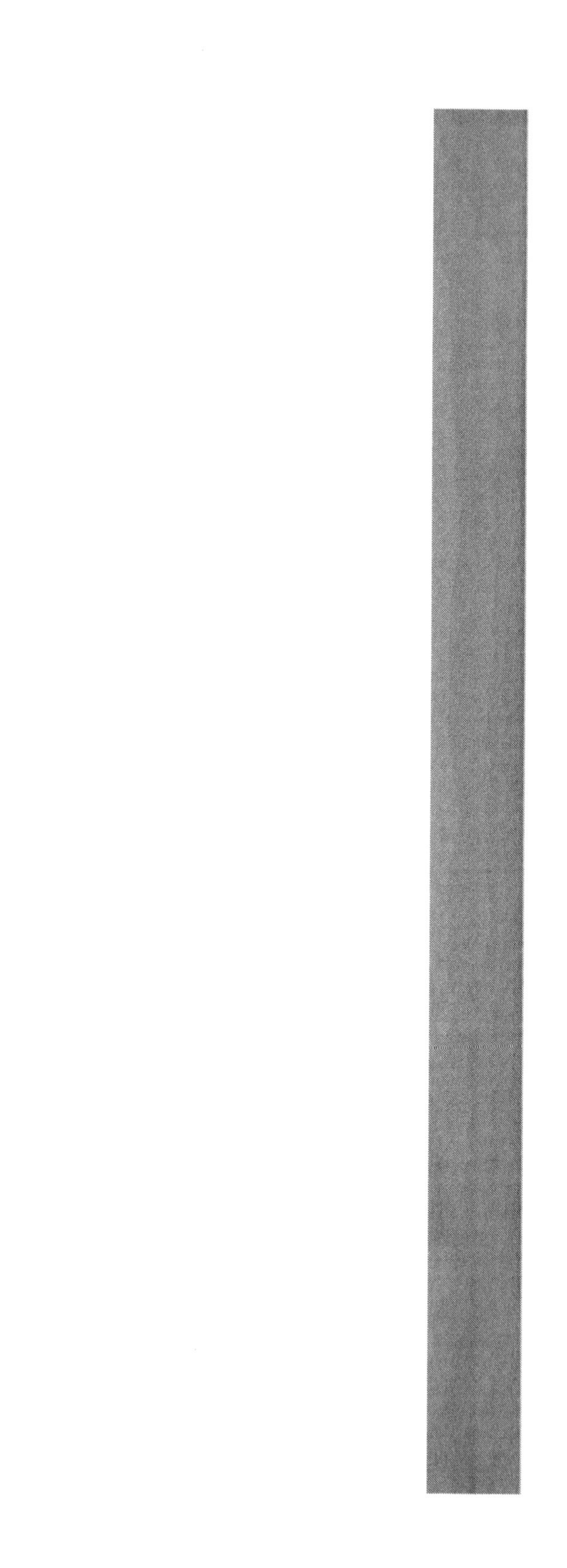